THE BEGINNING
OF OWNERSHIP

BY

THORSTEIN VEBLEN

British Library Cataloguing-in-Publication Data
A catalogue record for this book is available from the
British Library

Contents

Thorstein Veblen

Thorstein Bunde Veblen was born Torsten Bunde Veblen on 30th July 1857 in Cato, Wisconsin, United States, to Norwegian immigrant parents.

Veblen grew up on his parents farm in Nerstrand, Minnesota. This area and others like it were known as little Norways due to the religious and cultural traditions that had been imported from the old country. Although Norwegian was his first language, the young Veblen learned English from neighbours and at school.

His parents put a lot of emphasis on education and hard work and at age seventeen he was sent to study at Carleton College Academy. It was there that he met John Bates Clark (1847–1938) who went on to become a leader in the new field of neoclassical economics. Upon graduating Veblen conducted graduate work under Charles Sanders Pierce (the founder of the pragmatist school in philosophy) at John Hopkins University. He then moved to Yale in 1884 to take a Ph.D. and completed his dissertation on "Ethical Grounds of a Doctrine of Retribution."

Upon leaving Yale he was unable to find a employment. This was partly due to prejudice against Norwegians, and partly because most universities considered him insufficiently educated in Christianity; most academics at the time held divinity degrees. Due to this, Veblen returned to the family farm – ostensibly to recover from malaria – and spent six years there reading voraciously. However, in 1891 he was accepted to study economics as a graduate student at Cornell University. From here on his academic career took off, obtaining his first professional appointment at the University of Chicago – where in 1900 he was promoted to assistant professor – and from there moving on work at institutions including Stanford University and the University of Missouri.

Veblen drew from the work of 19th century intellectuals such as Charles Darwin and Herbert Spencer to develop a 20th century theory of evolutionary economics. He described economic behaviour as socially determined and saw economic organization as a process of ongoing evolution. In his work *The Theory of the Leisure Class* (1899) he outlined how rich and poor alike, attempt to impress others and seek to gain advantage through what Veblen coined "conspicuous consumption" and the ability to engage in "conspicuous leisure." In *The Theory of Business Enterprise* (1904) he used evolutionary analysis to explain the growth of business combinations and trusts.

In the 21st century his ideas have come back into the spotlight as a valid approach for studying the intricacies of economic systems and his theory that humans do not rationally pursue value and utility is one of the cornerstones of the modern discipline of behavioural economics. Veblen made a lasting contribution to his field and has influenced many scholars that have followed him.

Thorstein Veblen died in California on 3rd August 1929, less than three months before the crash of the U.S. Stock market crash which led to the great depression.

THE BEGINNING OF OWNERSHIP

BY

THORSTEIN VEBLEN AMERICAN JOURNAL OF SOCIOLOGY, VOL. 4 (1898-9)

In the accepted economic theories the ground of ownership is commonly conceived to be the productive labor of the owner. This is taken, without reflection or question, to be the legitimate basis of property; he who has produced a useful thing should possess and enjoy it. On this head the socialists and the economists of the classical line - the two extremes of economic speculation - are substantially at one. The point is not in controversy, or at least it has not been until recently; it has been accepted as an axiomatic premise. With the socialists it has served as the ground of their demand that the laborer should receive the full product of his labor. To classical economists the axiom has, perhaps, been as much trouble as it has been worth. It has given them no end of bother to explain how the capitalist is the "producer" of the goods that pass into his possession, and how it is true that the laborer gets what he produces. Sporadic instances of ownership quite dissociated from creative industry are recognized and taken account of as departures from the normal; they are due to disturbing causes. The main position is scarcely questioned, that in the normal case wealth is distributed in proportion to - and in some cogent sense because of - the recipient's contribution to the product.

Not only is the productive labor of the owner the definitive ground of his ownership today, but the derivation of the institution of property is similarly traced to the productive labor of that putative savage hunter who produced two deer or one beaver or twelve fish. The conjectural history of the origin of property, so far as it has been written by the economists, has been constructed out of conjecture proceeding on the preconceptions of Natural Rights and a coercive Order of Nature. To anyone who approaches the question of ownership with only an incidental interest in its solution (as is true of the classical, pre-evolutionary economists), and fortified with the preconceptions of natural rights, all this seems plain. It sufficiently accounts for the institution, both in point of logical derivation and in point of historical development. The "natural" owner is the person who has "produced" an article, or who, by a constructively equivalent expenditure of productive force, has found and appropriated an object. It is conceived that such a person becomes the owner of the article by virtue of the immediate logical inclusion of the idea of ownership under the idea of creative industry.

This natural-rights theory of property makes the creative effort of an isolated, self-sufficing individual the basis of the ownership vested in him. In so doing it overlooks the fact that there is no isolated, self-sufficing individual. All production is, in fact, a production in and by the help of the community, and all wealth is such only in society. Within the human period of the race development, it is safe to say, no individual has fallen into industrial isolation, so as to produce any one useful article by his own independent effort alone. Even where there is no mechanical co-operation, men are always guided by the experience of others. The only possible exceptions to this rule are those instances of lost or cast-off children nourished by wild beasts, of which half-authenticated accounts have gained currency from time to time. But the anomalous, half-hypothetical life of these waifs can scarcely have affected social development to the extent of originating the institution of ownership.

Production takes place only in society-only through the co-operation of an industrial community. This industrial community may be large or small; its limits are commonly somewhat vaguely defined; but it always comprises a group large enough to contain and transmit the traditions, tools, technical knowledge, and usages without which there can be no industrial organization and no economic relation of individuals to one another or to their environment. The isolated individual is not a productive agent. What he can do at best is to live from season to season, as the non-gregarious animals do. There can be no production without technical knowledge; hence no accumulation and no wealth to be owned, in severalty or otherwise. And there is no technical knowledge apart from an industrial community. Since there is no individual production and no individual productivity, the natural-rights preconception that ownership rests on the individually productive labor of the owner reduces itself to absurdity, even under the logic of its own assumptions.

Some writers who have taken up the question from the ethnological side hold that the institution is to be traced to the customary use of weapons and ornaments by individuals. Others have found its origin in the social group's occupation of a given piece of land, which it held forcibly against intruders, and which it came in this way to "own." The latter hypothesis bases the collective ownership of land on a collective act of seizure, or tenure by prowess, so that it differs fundamentally from the view which bases ownership on productive labor.

The view that ownership is an outgrowth of the customary consumption of such things as weapons and ornaments by individuals is well supported by appearances and has also the qualified sanction of the natural-rights preconception. The usages of all known primitive tribes seem at first sight to bear out this view. In all communities the individual members exercise a more or less unrestrained right of use and abuse over their weapons, if they have any, as well as over many articles of ornament, clothing, and the toilet. In the eyes of the modern economist this usage would count as ownership. So that, if the question is construed to be simply a question of material fact, as to the earliest emergence of usages which would in the latter-day classification be brought under the head of ownership, then it would have to be said that ownership must have begun with the conversion of these articles to individual use. But the question will have to be answered in the contrary sense if we shift our ground to the point of view of the primitive men whose institutions are under review. The point in question is the origin of the institution of ownership, as it first takes shape in the habits of thought of the early barbarian. The question concerns the derivation of the idea of ownership or property. What is of interest for the present purpose is not whether we, with our preconceptions, would look upon the relation of the primitive savage or barbarian to his slight personal effects as a relation of ownership, but whether that is his own apprehension of the matter. It is a question as to the light in which the savage himself habitually views these objects that pertain immediately to his person and are set apart for his habitual use. Like all questions of the derivation of institutions, it is essentially a question of folk-psychology, not of mechanical fact; and, when so conceived, it must be answered in the negative.

The unsophisticated man, whether savage or civilized, is prone to conceive phenomena in terms of personality; these being terms with which he has a first-hand acquaintance. This habit is more unbroken in the savage than in civilized men. All obvious manifestations of force are apprehended as expressions of conation - effort put forth for a purpose by some agency similar to the human will. The point of view of the archaic culture is that of forceful, pervading personality, whose unfolding life is the substantial fact held in view in every relation into which men or things enter. This point of view in large measure shapes and colors all the institutions of the early culture -and in a less degree the later phases of culture. Under the guidance of this habit of thought, the relation of any individual to his personal effects is conceived to be of a more intimate kind than that of ownership simply. Ownership is too external and colorless a term to describe the fact.

In the apprehension of the savage and the barbarian the limits of his person do not coincide with the limits which modern biological science would recognize. His individuality is conceived to cover, somewhat vaguely and uncertainly, a pretty wide fringe of facts and objects that pertain to him more or less immediately. To our sense of the matter these items lie outside the limits of his person, and to many of them we would conceive him to stand in an economic rather than in an organic relation. This quasi-personal fringe of facts and objects commonly comprises the man's shadow; the reflection of his image in water or any similar surface; his name; his peculiar tattoo marks; his totem, if he has one; his glance; his breath, especially when it is visible; the print of his hand and foot; the sound of his voice; any image or representation of his person; any excretions or exhalations from his person; parings of his nails; cuttings of his hair; his ornaments and amulets; clothing that is in daily use, especially what has been shaped to his person, and more particularly if there is wrought into it any totemic or other design peculiar to him; his weapons, especially his favorite weapons and those which he habitually carries. Beyond these there is a great number of other, remoter things which may or may not be included in the quasi-personal fringe.

As regards this entire range of facts and objects, it is to be said that the "zone of influence" of the individual's personality is not conceived to cover them all with the same degree of potency; his individuality shades off by insensible, penumbral gradations into the external world. The objects and facts that fall within the quasi-personal fringe figure in the habits of thought of the savage as personal to him in a vital sense. They are not a congeries of things to which he stands in an economic relation and to which he has an equitable, legal claim. These articles are conceived to be his in much the same sense as his hands and feet are his, or his pulse-beat, or his digestion, or the heat of his body, or the motions of his limbs or brain.

For the satisfaction of any who may be inclined to question this view, appeal may be taken to the usages of almost any people. Some such notion of a pervasive personality, or a penumbra of personality, is implied, for instance, in the giving and keeping of presents and mementos. It is more indubitably present in the working of charms; in all sorcery; in the sacraments and similar devout observances; in such practices as the Tibetan prayer-wheel; in the adoration of relics, images, and symbols; in the almost universal veneration of consecrated places and structures; in astrology; in divination by means of hair-cuttings, nail-parings, photographs, etc. Perhaps the least debatable evidence of belief in such a quasi-personal fringe is afforded by the practices of sympathetic magic; and the practices are strikingly similar in substance the world over-from the love-charm to the sacrament. Their substantial ground is the belief that a desired effect can be wrought upon a given person through the means of some object lying within his quasi-personal fringe. The person who is approached in this way may be a fellow-mortal, or it may be some potent spiritual agent whose intercession is sought for good or ill. If the sorcerer or anyone who works a charm can in any way get at the "penumbra" of a person's individuality, as embodied in his fringe of quasi-personal facts, he will be able to work good or ill to the person to whom the fact or object pertains; and the magic rites performed to this end will work their effect with greater force and precision in proportion as the object which affords the point of attack is more intimately related to the person upon whom the effect is to be wrought. An economic relation, simply, does not afford a handle for sorcery. It may be set down that whenever the relation of a person to a given object is made use of for the purposes of sympathetic magic, the relation. is conceived to be something more vital than simple legal ownership.

Such meager belongings of the primitive savage as would under the nomenclature of a later day be classed as personal property are not thought of by him as his property at all; they pertain organically to his person. Of the things comprised in his quasi-personal fringe all do not pertain to him with the same degree of intimacy or persistency; but those articles which are more remotely or more doubtfully included under his individuality are not therefore conceived to be partly organic to him and partly his property simply. The alternative does not lie between this organic relation and ownership. It may easily happen that a given article lying along the margin of the quasi-personal fringe is eliminated from it and is alienated, either by default through lapse of time or by voluntary severance of the relation. But when this happens the article is not conceived to escape from the organic relation into a remoter category of things that are owned by and external to the person in question. If an object escapes in this way from the organic sphere of one person, it may pass into the sphere of another; or, if it is an article that lends itself to common use, it may pass into the common stock of the community.

As regards this common stock, no concept of ownership, either communal or individual, applies in the primitive community. The idea of a communal ownership is of relatively late growth, and must by psychological necessity have been preceded by the idea of individual ownership. Ownership is an accredited discretionary power over an object on the ground of a conventional claim; it implies that the owner is a personal agent who takes thought for the disposal of the object owned. A personal agent is an individual, and it is only by an eventual refinement - of the nature of a legal fiction - that any group of men is conceived to exercise a corporate discretion over objects. Ownership implies an individual owner. It is only by reflection, and by extending the scope of a concept which is already familiar, that a quasi-personal corporate discretion and control of this kind comes to be imputed to a group of persons. Corporate ownership is quasi-ownership only; it is therefore necessarily a derivative concept, and cannot have preceded the concept of individual ownership of which it is a counterfeit.

After the idea of ownership has been elaborated and has gained some consistency, it is not unusual to find the notion of pervasion by the user's personality applied to articles owned by him. At the same time a given article may also be recognized as lying within the quasi-personal fringe of one person while it is owned by another - as, for instance, ornaments and other articles of daily use which in a personal sense belong to a slave or to an inferior member of a patriarchal household, but which as property belong to the master or head of the household. The two categories, (a) things to which one's personality extends by way of pervasion and (b) things owned, by no means coincide; nor does the one supplant the other. The two ideas are so far from identical that the same object may belong to one person under the one concept and to another person under the other; and, on the other hand, the same person may stand in both relations to a given object without the one concept being lost in the other. A given article may change owners without passing out of the quasi-personal fringe of the person under whose "self" it has belonged, as, for instance, a photograph or any other memento. A familiar instance is the mundane ownership of any consecrated place or structure which in the personal sense belongs to the saint or deity to whom it is sacred.

The two concepts are so far distinct, or even disparate, as to make it extremely improbable that the one has been developed out of the other by a process of growth.

A transition involving such a substitution of ideas could scarcely take place except on some notable impulse from without. Such a step would amount to the construction of a new category and a reclassification of certain selected facts under the new head. The impulse to reclassify the facts and things that are comprised in the quasi-personal fringe, so as to place some of them, together with certain other things, under the new category of ownership, must come from some constraining exigency of later growth than the concept whose province it invades. The new category is not simply an amplified form of the old. Not every item that was originally conceived to belong to an individual by way of pervasion comes to be counted as an item of his wealth after the idea of wealth has come into vogue. Such items, for instance, as a person's footprint, or his image or effigy, or his name, are very tardily included under the head of articles owned by him, if they are eventually included at all. It is a fortuitous circumstance if they come to be owned by him, but they long continue to hold their place in his quasi-personal fringe. The disparity of the two concepts is well brought out by the case of the domestic animals. These non-human individuals are incapable of ownership, but there is imputed to them the attribute of a pervasive individuality, which extends to such items as their footprints, their stalls, clippings of hair, and the like. These items are made use of for the purposes of sympathetic magic even in modern civilized communities. An illustration that may show this disparity between ownership and pervasion in a still stronger light is afforded by the vulgar belief that the moon's phases may have a propitious or sinister effect on human affairs. The inconstant moon is conceived to work good or ill through a sympathetic influence or spiritual infection which suggests a quasi-personal fringe, but which assuredly does not imply ownership on her part.

Ownership is not a simple and instinctive notion that is naively included under the notion of productive effort on the one hand, nor under that of habitual use on the other. It is not something given to begin with, as an item of the isolated individual's mental furniture; something which has to be unlearned in part when men come to co-operate in production and make working arrangements and mutual renunciations under the stress of associated life - after the manner imputed by the social-contract theory. It is a conventional fact and has to be learned; it is a cultural fact which has grown into an institution in the past through a long course of habituation, and which is transmitted from generation to generation as all cultural facts are.

On going back a little way into the cultural history of our own past, we come upon a situation which says that the fact of a person's being engaged in industry was prima facie evidence that he could own nothing. Under serfdom and slavery those who work cannot own, and those who own cannot work. Even very recently - culturally speaking - there was no suspicion that a woman's work, in the patriarchal household, should entitle her to own the products of her work. Farther back in the barbarian culture, while the patriarchal household was in better preservation than it is now, this position was accepted with more unquestioning faith. The head of the household alone could hold property; and even the scope of his ownership was greatly qualified if he had a feudal superior. The tenure of property is a tenure by prowess, on the one hand, and a tenure by sufferance at the hands of a superior, on the other hand. The recourse to prowess as the definitive basis of tenure becomes more immediate and more habitual the farther the development is traced back into the early barbarian culture; until, on the lower levels of barbarism or the upper levels of savagery, "the good old plan" prevails with but little mitigation. There are always certain conventions, a certain understanding as to what are the legitimate conditions and circumstances that surround ownership and its transmission, chief among which is the fact of habitual acceptance. What has been currently accepted as the status quo-vested interest - is right and good so long as it does not meet a challenge backed by irresistible force. Property rights sanctioned by immemorial usage are inviolable, as all immemorial usage is, except in the face of forcible dispossession. But seizure and forcible retention very shortly gain the legitimation of usage, and the resulting tenure becomes inviolable through habituation. Beati possidentes.

Throughout the barbarian culture, where this tenure by prowess prevails, the population falls into two economic classes: those engaged in industrial employments, and those engaged in such non-industrial pursuits as war, government, sports, and religious observances. In the earlier and more naive stages of barbarism the former, in the normal case, own nothing; the latter own such property as they have seized, or such as has, under the sanction of usage, descended upon them from their forebears who seized and held it. At a still lower level of culture, in the primitive savage horde, the population is not similarly divided into economic classes. There is no leisure class resting its prerogative on coercion, prowess, and immemorial status; and there is also no ownership.

It will hold as a rough generalization that in communities where there is no invidious distinction between employments, as exploit, on the one hand, and drudgery, on the other, there is also no tenure of property. In the cultural sequence, ownership does not begin before the rise of a canon of exploit; but it is to be added that it also does not seem to begin with the first beginning of exploit as a manly occupation. In these very rude early communities, especially in the unpropertied hordes of peaceable savages, the rule is that the product of any member's effort is consumed by the group to which he belongs; and it is consumed collectively or indiscriminately, without question of individual right or ownership. The question of ownership is not brought up by the fact that an article has been produced or is at hand in finished form for consumption.

The earliest occurrence of ownership seems to fall in the early stages of barbarism, and the emergence of the institution of ownership is apparently a concomitant of the transition from a peaceable to a predatory habit of life. It is a prerogative of that class in the barbarian culture which leads a life of exploit rather than of industry. The pervading characteristic of the barbarian culture, as distinguished from the peaceable phase of life that precedes it, is the element of exploit, coercion, and seizure. In its earlier phases ownership is this habit of coercion and seizure reduced to system and consistency under the surveillance of usage.

The practice of seizing and accumulating goods on individual account could not have come into vogue to the extent of founding a new institution under the peaceable communistic regime of primitive savagery; for the dissensions arising from any such resort to mutual force and fraud among its members would have been fatal to the group. For a similar reason individual ownership of consumable goods could not come in with the first beginnings of predatory life; for the primitive fighting horde still needs to consume its scanty means of subsistence in common, in order to give the collective horde its full fighting efficiency. Otherwise it would succumb before any rival horde that had not yet given up collective consumption.

With the advent of predatory life comes the practice of plundering - of seizing goods from the enemy. But in order that the plundering habit should give rise to individual ownership of the things seized, these things must be goods of a somewhat lasting kind, and not immediately consumable means of subsistence. Under the primitive culture the means of subsistence are habitually consumed in common by the group, and the manner in which such goods are consumed is fixed according to an elaborate system of usage. This usage is not readily broken over, for it is a substantial part of the habits of life of every individual member. The practice of collective consumption is at the same time necessary to the survival of the group, and this necessity is present in men's minds and exercises a surveillance over the formation of habits of thought as to what is right and seemly. Any propensity to aggression at this early stage will, therefore, not assert itself in the seizure and retention of consumable goods; nor does the temptation to do so readily present itself, since the idea of individual appropriation of a store of goods is alien to the archaic man's general habits of thought.

The idea of property is not readily attached to anything but tangible and lasting articles. It is only where commercial development is well advanced - where bargain and sale is a large feature in the community's life-that the more perishable articles of consumption are thought of as items of wealth at all. The still more evanescent results of personal service are still more difficult to bring in under the idea of wealth. So much so that the attempt to classify services as wealth is meaningless to laymen, and even the adept economists hold a divided opinion as to the intelligibility of such a classification. In the common-sense apprehension the idea of property is not currently attached to any but tangible, vendible goods of some durability. This is true even in modern civilized communities, where pecuniary ideas and the pecuniary point of view prevail. In a like manner and for a like reason, in an earlier, non-commercial phase of culture there is less occasion for and greater difficulty in applying the concept of ownership to anything but obviously durable articles.

But durable articles of use and consumption which are seized in the raids of a predatory horde are either articles of general use or they are articles of immediate and continued personal use to the person who has seized them. In the former case the goods are consumed in common by the group, without giving rise to a notion of ownership; in the latter case they fall into the class of things that pertain organically to the person of their user, and they would, therefore, not figure as items of property or make up a store of wealth.

It is difficult to see how an institution of ownership could have arisen in the early days of predatory life through the seizure of goods, but the case is different with the seizure of persons. Captives are items that do not fit into the scheme of communal consumption, and their appropriation by their individual captor works no manifest detriment to the group. At the same time these captives continue to be obviously distinct from their captor in point of individuality, and so are not readily brought in under the quasi-personal fringe. The captives taken under rude conditions are chiefly women. There are good reasons for this. Except where there is a slave class of men, the women are more useful, as well as more easily controlled, in the primitive group. Their labor is worth more to the group than their maintenance, and as they do not carry weapons, they are less formidable than men captives would be. They serve the purpose of trophies very effectually, and it is therefore worth while for their captor to trace and keep in evidence his relation to them as their captor. To this end he maintains an attitude of dominance and coercion toward women captured by him; and, as being the insignia of his prowess, he does not suffer them to stand at the beck and call of rival warriors. They are fit subjects for command and constraint; it ministers to both his honor and his vanity to domineer over them, and their utility in this respect is very great. But his domineering over them is the evidence of his prowess, and it is incompatible with their utility as trophies that other men should take the liberties with his women which serve as evidence of the coercive relation of captor.

When the practice hardens into custom, the captor comes to exercise a customary right to exclusive use and abuse over the women he has seized; and this customary right of use and abuse over an object which is obviously not an organic part of his person constitutes the relation of ownership, as naively apprehended. After this usage of capture has found its way into the habits of the community, the women so held in constraint and in evidence will commonly fall into a conventionally recognized marriage relation with their captor. The result is a new form of marriage, in which the man is master. This ownership-marriage seems to be the original both of private property and of the patriarchal household. Both of these great institutions are, accordingly, of an emulative origin.

The varying details of the development whereby ownership extends to other persons than captured women cannot be taken up here; neither can the further growth of the marriage institution that came into vogue at the same time with ownership. Probably at a point in the economic evolution not far subsequent to the definitive installation of the institution of ownership-marriage comes, as its consequence, the ownership of consumable goods. The women held in servile marriage not only render personal service to their master, but they are also employed in the production of articles of use. All the noncombatant or ignoble members of the community are habitually so employed. And when the habit of looking upon and claiming the persons identified with my invidious interest, or subservient to me, as "mine" has become an accepted and integral part of men's habits of thought, it becomes a relatively easy matter to extend this newly achieved concept of ownership to the products of the labor performed by the persons so held in ownership. And the same propensity for emulation which bears so great a part in shaping the original institution of ownership extends its action to the new category of things owned. Not only are the products of the women's labor claimed and valued for their serviceability in furthering the comfort and fullness of life of the master, but they are valuable also as a conspicuous evidence of his possessing many and efficient servants, and they are therefore useful as an evidence of his superior force. The appropriation and accumulation of consumable goods could scarcely have come into vogue as a direct outgrowth of the primitive horde-communism, but it comes in as an easy and unobtrusive consequence of the ownership of persons.

www.ingramcontent.com/pod-product-compliance
Lightning Source LLC
Chambersburg PA
CBHW021340290326
41933CB00038B/994